CW00821161

by Iain Gray

Lang**Syne**

PUBLISHING

WRITING *to* REMEMBER

Lang**Syne**

PUBLISHING

WRITING *to* REMEMBER

Strathclyde Business Centre
120 Carstairs Street, Glasgow G40 4JD
Tel: 0141 554 9944 Fax: 0141 554 9955
E-mail: info@scottish-memories.co.uk
www.langsyneshop.co.uk

Design by Dorothy Meikle
Printed by Hay Nisbet Press, Glasgow
© Lang Syne Publishers Ltd 2008

ISBN 1-85217-273-8

Reilly

MOTTO:
Fortitude and prudence.

CREST:
An oak tree entwined with a serpent.

NAME variations include:
Ó Raghailligh *(Gaelic)*, Riley,
O'Reilly, Rahilly, Raleigh.

Chapter one:
Origins of Irish surnames

**According to an old saying, there are two types of Irish –
those who actually are Irish and those who wish they were.**

This sentiment is only one example of the allure that the
high romance and drama of the proud nation's history holds
for thousands of people scattered across the world today.

It's a sad fact, however, that the vast majority of Irish
surnames are found far beyond Irish shores, rather than on
the Emerald Isle itself.

The population stood at around eight million souls in
1841, but today it stands at fewer than six million.

This is mainly a tragic consequence of the potato
famine, also known as the Great Hunger, which devastated
Ireland between 1845 and 1849.

The Irish peasantry had become almost wholly reliant
for basic sustenance on the potato, first introduced from the
Americas in the seventeenth century.

When the crop was hit by a blight, at least 800,000
people starved to death while an estimated two million
others were forced to seek a new life far from their native
shores – particularly in America, Canada, and Australia.

The effects of the potato blight continued until about
1851, by which time a firm pattern of emigration had
become established.

Ireland's loss, however, was to the gain of the countries in which the immigrants settled, contributing enormously, as their descendants do today, to the well being of the nations in which their forefathers settled.

But those who were forced through dire circumstance to establish a new life in foreign parts never forgot their roots, or the proud heritage and traditions of the land that gave them birth.

Nor do their descendants.

It is a heritage that is inextricably bound up in the colourful variety of Irish names themselves – and the origin and history of these names forms an integral part of the vibrant drama that is the nation's history, one of both glorious fortune and tragic misfortune.

This history is well documented, and one of the most important and fascinating of the earliest sources are *The Annals of the Four Masters*, compiled between 1632 and 1636 by four friars at the Franciscan Monastery in County Donegal.

Compiled from earlier sources, and purporting to go back to the Biblical Deluge, much of the material takes in the mythological origins and history of Ireland and the Irish.

This includes tales of successive waves of invaders and settlers such as the Fomorians, the Partholonians, the Nemedians, the Fir Bolgs, the Tuatha De Danann, and the Laigain.

Of particular interest are the *Milesian Genealogies*,

because the majority of Irish clans today claim a descent from either Heremon, Ir, or Heber – three of the sons of Milesius, a king of what is now modern day Spain.

These sons invaded Ireland in the second millennium B.C, apparently in fulfilment of a mysterious prophecy received by their father.

This Milesian lineage is said to have ruled Ireland for nearly 3,000 years, until the island came under the sway of England's King Henry II in 1171 following what is known as the Cambro-Norman invasion.

This is an important date not only in Irish history in general, but for the effect the invasion subsequently had for Irish surnames.

'Cambro' comes from the Welsh, and 'Cambro-Norman' describes those Welsh knights of Norman origin who invaded Ireland.

But they were invaders who stayed, inter-marrying with the native Irish population and founding their own proud dynasties that bore Cambro-Norman names such as Archer, Barbour, Brannagh, Fitzgerald, Fitzgibbon, Fleming, Joyce, Plunkett, and Walsh – to name only a few.

These 'Cambro-Norman' surnames that still flourish throughout the world today form one of the three main categories in which Irish names can be placed – those of Gaelic-Irish, Cambro-Norman, and Anglo-Irish.

Previous to the Cambro-Norman invasion of the twelfth century, and throughout the earlier invasions and settlement of those wild bands of sea rovers known as the Vikings in the eighth and ninth centuries, the population of the island was relatively small, and it was normal for a person to be identified through the use of only a forename.

But as population gradually increased and there were many more people with the same forename, surnames were adopted to distinguish one person, or one community, from another.

Individuals identified themselves with their own particular tribe, or 'tuath', and this tribe – that also became known as a clann, or clan – took its name from some distinguished ancestor who had founded the clan.

The Gaelic-Irish form of the name Kelly, for example, is Ó Ceallaigh, or O'Kelly, indicating descent from an original 'Ceallaigh', with the 'O' denoting 'grandson of.' The name was later anglicised to Kelly.

The prefix 'Mac' or 'Mc', meanwhile, as with the clans of the Scottish Highlands, denotes 'son of.'

Although the Irish clans had much in common with their Scottish counterparts, one important difference lies in what are known as 'septs', or branches, of the clan.

Septs of Scottish clans were groups who often bore an entirely different name from the clan name but were under the clan's protection.

In Ireland, septs were groups that shared the same name and who could be found scattered throughout the four provinces of Ulster, Leinster, Munster, and Connacht.

The 'golden age' of the Gaelic-Irish clans, infused as their veins were with the blood of Celts, pre-dates the Viking invasions of the eighth and ninth centuries and the Norman invasion of the twelfth century, and the sacred heart of the country was the Hill of Tara, near the River Boyne, in County Meath.

Known in Gaelic as 'Teamhar na Rí', or Hill of Kings, it was the royal seat of the 'Ard Rí Éireann', or High King of Ireland, to whom the petty kings, or chieftains, from the island's provinces were ultimately subordinate.

It was on the Hill of Tara, beside a stone pillar known as the Irish 'Lia Fáil', or Stone of Destiny, that the High Kings were inaugurated and, according to legend, this stone would emit a piercing screech that could be heard all over Ireland when touched by the hand of the rightful king.

The Hill of Tara is today one of the island's main tourist attractions.

Opposition to English rule over Ireland, established in the wake of the Cambro-Norman invasion, broke out frequently and the harsh solution adopted by the powerful forces of the Crown was to forcibly evict the native Irish from their lands.

These lands were then granted to Protestant colonists, or 'planters', from Britain.

Many of these colonists, ironically, came from Scotland and were the descendants of the original 'Scotti', or 'Scots', who gave their name to Scotland after migrating there in the fifth century A.D., from the north of Ireland.

Colonisation entailed harsh penal laws being imposed on the majority of the native Irish population, stripping them practically of all of their rights.

The Crown's main bastion in Ireland was Dublin and its environs, known as the Pale, and it was the dispossessed peasantry who lived outside this Pale, desperately striving to eke out a meagre living.

It was this that gave rise to the modern-day expression of someone or something being 'beyond the pale'.

Attempts were made to stamp out all aspects of the ancient Gaelic-Irish culture, to the extent that even to bear a Gaelic-Irish name was to invite discrimination.

This is why many Gaelic-Irish names were anglicised with, for example, and noted above, Ó Ceallaigh, or O'Kelly, being anglicised to Kelly.

Succeeding centuries have seen strong revivals of Gaelic-Irish consciousness, however, and this has led to many families reverting back to the original form of their name, while the language itself is frequently found on the fluent tongues of an estimated 90,000 to 145,000 of the island's population.

Ireland's turbulent history of religious and political strife is one that lasted well into the twentieth century, a landmark century that saw the partition of the island into the twenty-six counties of the independent Republic of

Ireland, or Eire, and the six counties of Northern Ireland, or Ulster.

Dublin, originally founded by Vikings, is now a vibrant and truly cosmopolitan city while the proud city of Belfast is one of the jewels in the crown of Ulster.

It was Saint Patrick who first brought the light of Christianity to Ireland in the fifth century A.D.

Interpretations of this Christian message have varied over the centuries, often leading to bitter sectarian conflict – but the many intricately sculpted Celtic Crosses found all over the island are symbolic of a unity that crosses the sectarian divide.

It is an image that fuses the 'old gods' of the Celts with Christianity.

All the signs from the early years of this new millennium indicate that sectarian strife may soon become a thing of the past – with the Irish and their many kinsfolk across the world, be they Protestant or Catholic, finding common purpose in the rich tapestry of their shared heritage.

Chapter two:

Myth and legend

County Cavan, in the northern reaches of the present day Irish Republic, was for centuries the homeland of the proud clan of Reilly – a clan that can boast an ancient and illustrious pedigree that is entwined with the dramatic history of the island itself.

It is not known with any degree of certainty from where they originally hailed, but one curious tradition concerning the Reilly Coat of Arms points to the fact that it was certainly from 'beyond the sea.'

The Coat of Arms, with its motto of 'Fortitude and prudence' and crest of an oak tree entwined with a serpent, also features a severed hand dripping blood.

According to the rather gruesome tradition, this refers to the fact that when approaching the Irish coast, a father had told his two sons that whoever touched land first would be granted his choice of territory.

Racing across the sea in their boats one of the brothers began to lag behind the other. Determined that he would be the first to 'touch' Irish soil, he chopped off his hand and threw it ashore ahead of his brother.

The Irish Gaelic form of Reilly is Ó Raghailligh, indicating descent from Raghallach who, in turn, was descended from Maelmorda.

This is why the Reilly territory in present day Co. Cavan was known as Muinter Maelmorda – 'the country of Maelmorda's people.'

The area controlled by the Reillys, centred on Balleyjamesduff, was also known as Breifne O'Reilly, or East Breifne, with the territory controlled by their neighbours and great rivals the O'Rourkes known as Breifne O'Rourke – now Co. Leitrim.

This territorial division had resulted from a fierce battle fought in 1256 between the O'Reillys and the O'Rourkes at Ballinamore.

'Ó Raghailligh' means 'gregarious race', and it was on the Hill of Shantoman and later on the Hill of Tullymongan that the chieftains of this 'gregarious race' were inaugurated in ancient and solemn ceremony.

To this day, the ruins of what is thought to have been a Druid temple can still be seen on the Hill of Shantoman.

The temple is in the form of several huge standing stones known as Fionn McCool's Fingers – referring to the mythological Irish hero also known as Fionn MacCumhail, leader of the legendary band of warriors known as the Fianna, or Fenians.

Another legendary Irish hero, and one to whom the Reillys of today are entitled to claim a descent, is the gloriously named Conn Céthchathach, the Gaelic form for Conn of the Hundred Battles, with 'Conn' signifying 'great wisdom.'

Ard Rí, or High King of Ireland from about 177 to 212 A.D. this progenitor, or ancestor, of the Reillys and other native Irish clans, figures prominently in what are known as the Fenian Cycle of tales, also known as the Ossianic Cycle and thought to date from the third century.

One of Conn's illustrious ancestors is said to have been no less than Goidel Glas, who is reputed to have created the Gaelic-Irish language after he combined and refined the 72 known languages of his time.

The result is the language of poets that thrills like the plucked strings of an Irish harp throughout the Fenian Cycle.

As a youth, Conn is said to have met two mysterious figures who predicted he and his descendants would rule Ireland.

The strange figures who are reputed by legend to have appeared to Conn, enshrouded in mist, were a beautiful young maiden known as Sovranty; wearing a golden crown and seated on a crystal chair, she was accompanied by the sun god Lugh, patron of arts and crafts.

It is said they prophesied his descendants would rule until the death of the old Gods – which in fact did occur in the form of St. Patrick and the new religious pantheon of Christianity.

Conn attained the High Kingship after overthrowing Cathair Mór, also known as Mal, who had killed his father.

But his kingship was never secure because he had to

fight a relentless succession of battles with his great rival Eogan Mór, also known as Mug Nadhat, king of the Dál nAraide, or Cruithe, who occupied the northeastern territories of Ireland.

It was because of the number of battles Conn fought with these Cruithne, or Picts, that he earned the title of Conn Céthchathach – Conn of the Hundred Battles.

The two rival kings achieved a temporary accommodation after the island was divided between themselves, the division starting at a ridge known as Eiscir Riada, which traverses the island from Galway Bay to Dublin.

Mug's territory in the south was known as Leth Moga Nuadht, while Conn's northern territory was known as Leth Cuinn.

But it was not long before the ambitious and fiercely proud pair were at each other's throats again.

Mug gained the upper hand for a time after storing up grain in his territories after taking heed of a dire Druidic prophecy of famine – but Conn eventually defeated his rival after taking him by cunning surprise in a night raid near present-day Tullamore, in County Offaly.

Conn consolidated his kingship over Ireland, but his success was short-lived, destined to die under the glinting blades of fifty warriors who had managed to breach the defences of his royal bastion of Tara after disguising themselves as women.

At the head of these warriors was the vengeful Tibride Tirech, son of the Cathair Mór whom Conn had killed years earlier in revenge for the death of his own father.

A fourth century A.D. descendant of Conn was Brian, a king of the province of Connacht; his descendants became known as the Ui Briuin –the race of Brian – and it was Feargna, one of his 24 sons, who was the grandfather of Maelmorda.

This Maelmorda, in turn, was the father of the Raghallach from whom the Reillys take their name.

It is through Raghallach that the Reillys of today can claim a link to one of the greatest and most decisive battles ever fought on Irish soil.

This was the battle of Clontarf, fought about four miles north of Dublin on Good Friday of 1014.

Late tenth and early eleventh century Ireland was the scene of vicious inter-clan rivalry as successive clan chiefs fought for supremacy over their rivals.

It was this disunity that worked to the advantage of the Norman invaders of the late twelfth century and the Viking invaders of previous centuries.

The period 795 A.D. to 1014 A.D. is known to Irish history as The Viking Tyranny, and it was largely through the inspired leadership of the great Irish hero king Brian Boru that Viking power was diminished, although not completely eliminated.

Boru was able to achieve this by managing to rally a

number of other chieftains to his cause – although by no means all.

Boru, also known as Brian Bóruma and the ancestor of the distinguished O'Brien clan, was a son of Cennetig, king of Dál Cais, in the northern reaches of the province of Munster.

With his battle-hardened warriors known as the Dalcassian knights at his side, Boru had by 1002 A.D. achieved the prize of the High Kingship of Ireland – but there were still rival chieftains, and not least the Vikings, to deal with.

These Vikings, known as Ostmen, had occupied and fortified Dublin in the mid-ninth century and had other important trading settlements on other parts of the island.

Resenting Brian Boru's High Kingship, a number of chieftains, particularly those of the province of Leinster, found common cause with the Ostmen, and the two sides met in final and bloody confrontation at Clontarf.

Boru proved victorious, but the annals speak of great slaughter on the day, with the dead piled high on the field of battle; hundreds of other Ostmen drowned after they fled the field of carnage to seek the safety of their longships.

But Boru had little time to celebrate his victory – being killed in his tent by a party of fleeing Vikings, but not before felling most of them with his great two-handed sword.

While there is a persistent Reilly tradition that their great ancestor Raghallach was on the field of battle at Clontarf, one problem is that it is not known with certainty on whose side he actually fought!

Shrewd self interest had dictated what side the numerous clan chieftains took in the conflict, and Raghallach cannot be blamed if he had sided with the Ostmen if by doing so it would have served the best interests of his kith and kin.

The likelihood, however, is that he had indeed fought at the side of the hero king Brian Boru.

Chapter three:
The life of Reilly

What would ultimately prove to be the death knell of the ancient way of life of native Irish clans such as the Reillys was sounded by the late twelfth century Cambro-Norman invasion of Ireland, followed by its consolidation under an Anglo-Norman invasion.

English dominion over the island was ratified through the Treaty of Windsor of 1175, under the terms of which chieftains were only allowed to rule territory unoccupied by the Normans in the role of a vassal of the English king.

What was gradually created were three separate 'Irelands.'

There were the territories of the privileged and powerful Norman barons and their retainers, the Ireland of the disaffected Gaelic-Irish such as the Reillys, and the Pale – comprised of Dublin itself and a substantial area of its environs ruled over by an English elite.

A simmering cauldron of discontent and resentment had been created – one that would boil over periodically in subsequent centuries with particularly dire consequences for the Reillys and other Irish clans.

In 1641 the Catholic landowners rebelled such as the Reillys against the English Crown's policy of settling, or 'planting' loyal Protestants on Irish land.

This policy had started during the reign from 1491 to 1547 of Henry VIII, whose Reformation effectively outlawed the established Roman Catholic faith throughout his dominions.

This settlement of loyal Protestants in Ireland continued throughout the subsequent reigns of Elizabeth I, James I (James VI of Scotland), and Charles I.

In the insurrection that exploded in 1641, at least 2,000 Protestant settlers were massacred at the hands of Catholic landowners and their native Irish peasantry, while thousands more were stripped of their belongings and driven from their lands to seek refuge where they could.

Among the leaders of the rebellion in present day Co. Cavan was Myles O'Reilly, better known to posterity by the rather more frightening name of Myles the Slasher.

In one particularly vicious encounter at Belturbet he had 60 hapless English settlers thrown over a bridge to drown in the river below; in the sickening tit-for-tat retaliation of the times, this only served to provoke revenge from the English forces in the form of 27 Irish natives being summarily put to the sword and 14 others hanged from the nearest trees.

The bold Myles the Slasher himself, keen-edged sword still in hand, was killed in 1644 while attempting to defend a vital river crossing.

Terrible as the atrocities against the Protestant settlers had undoubtedly been, subsequent accounts became greatly exaggerated, serving to fuel a burning desire on the part of Protestants for revenge against the rebels.

Tragically for Ireland, this revenge became directed not only against the rebels in particular, but native Irish Catholics such as the Reillys in general.

The English Civil War intervened to prevent immediate action against the rebels, but following the execution of Charles I in 1649 and the consolidation of the power of England's fanatically Protestant Oliver Cromwell, the time was ripe for revenge.

The Lord Protector, as he was named, descended on Ireland at the head of a 20,000-strong army that landed at Ringford, near Dublin, in August of 1649.

The consequences of this Cromwellian conquest still resonate throughout the island today.

Cromwell had three main aims: to quash all forms of rebellion, to 'remove' all Catholic landowners who had taken part in the rebellion, and to convert the native Irish to the Protestant faith.

An early warning of the terrors that were in store for the native Catholic Irish came when the northeastern town of Drogheda was stormed and taken in September and between 2,000 and 4,000 of its inhabitants killed, including priests who were summarily put to the sword.

It was not long before Cromwell held Ireland in a grip of iron, allowing him to implement what amounted to a policy of ethnic cleansing.

His troopers were given free rein to hunt down and kill

priests, while Catholic estates such as those of the Reillys were confiscated.

Many native Irish were forced to seek refuge on foreign shores, including Colonel Myles O'Reilly, who had served as a dashing and daring rebel cavalry officer.

He fled into exile in Spain in 1653.

More than 30 years later, in the wake of the 'Glorious Revolution' that brought the Protestant William of Orange and his wife Mary to the throne and the flight into exile of the Catholic monarch James II (James VII of Scotland), Hugh Reilly of Cavan was also forced into exile.

Under James, he had held the powerful posts of Master of Chancery and Clerk of the King's Council for Ireland.

Another Reilly who had fought for the cause of the Stuart monarch James II in what is known as The War of the Two Kings, was Colonel John Reilly, a son of the infamous Myles the Slasher.

He was allowed to keep his lands under the terms of the Treaty of Limerick of October 1691, but his grandson, Alexander O'Reilly, born in Baltrasna, Co. Meath, in 1722 was destined to achieve fame on foreign shores as Count Alejandro Reilly.

Leaving his native land he joined the forces of the famed Irish Brigade serving the military cause of Spain.

By 1765 he had attained the rank of Field Marshall and was despatched to what was then the Spanish possession of Puerto Rico to establish a force of people's militia.

That is why to this day he is known as 'the father of the Puerto Rican militia.'

Four years later, in 1769, he was governor of colonial Louisiana, taking formal possession of the former French territory in the name of Spain. He died in 1794.

Born in 1823 in Monaghan Town, Thomas Devin Reilly was the Irish republican and revolutionary who fled to the United States following his involvement in the abortive Young Irelander Rebellion of 1848.

'Young Irelanders' such as Reilly had advocated the non-payment of rents and the tearing up of railway lines in a desperate bid to stop the removal of vital food supplies from the island during the terrible time from 1845 to 1849 known as the Great Hunger, caused by the failure of the potato crop.

Reilly continued to advocate the cause of Irish independence from his American exile, until his death in 1854.

During the medieval period the Reillys had also become noted as successful traders and merchants – to the extent that Irish money was known as a 'reilly.'

It is thought that the well-known phrase to 'lead the life of Reilly' stems from the affluence and comforts the Reillys once enjoyed.

While the notorious Myles the Slasher and other Reillys made a name for themselves on the battlefield, other Reillys achieved distinction as noted churchmen – having to date produced at least eight Irish bishops and five Primates of All-Ireland.

Chapter four:
On the world stage

Generations of Reillys, in all the rich variety of spellings of the surname, have achieved fame in a wide and colourful variety of pursuits.

On the silver screen, **John C. Reilly**, born in Chicago in 1965, is the actor who achieved the accolade in 2002 of being nominated for no less than three Academy Awards.

These were for his roles in the musical *Chicago*, *Gangs of New York*, and *The Hours* – winning the award for Best Supporting Actor in Chicago.

Reilly, whose first film role was in the 1989 *Casualties of War*, also appeared in the 2004 movie *The Aviator*, based on the life of American tycoon Howard Hughes.

Born in 1977, **Kelly Reilly** is the English actress who in 2004 was an Olivier Awards nominee for Best Actress for her role in *After Miss Julie*, while a year later she won the Cannes Film Festival award for Best Actress in an Independent Film for her performance in *Mrs Henderson Presents*.

An accomplished actor on both stage and film, **Charles Nelson Reilly** is also a director and drama teacher and the recipient of a prestigious Tony Award for his performance in the 1962 production of *How To Succeed In Business Without Really Trying*.

Born in Los Angeles in 1980, **Cassia Riley** is the

glamorous model who was a Penthouse Pet of the Month in 2005 and Pet of the Year runner-up in 2006, while **Bill O'Reilly**, born in New York City in 1949, is the often controversial television presenter best known as host of the Fox News Channel's *The O'Reilly Factor*.

He is also an author and syndicated newspaper columnist.

James E. Reilly, born in Bountiful, Utah, in 1948, is the prolific writer of popular American soap operas that to date have included *The Young and the Restless*, *Days Of Our Lives*, and *Guiding Light*.

In the world of music, **Ben Riley**, born in Savannah, Georgia, in 1933, is the jazz drummer whose rather unlikely introduction to music was playing in a U.S. Army band while serving as a paratrooper in the early 1950s.

Since he began his professional career in 1956, he has played with a range of jazz greats that have included Alice Coltrane, Thelonius Monk, Woody Herman, Sten Getz, Woody "Lockjaw" Davis, and Kenny Baron.

Along with Baron, he was a member of the band Sphere.

Toronto-born **Doug Riley** is the Canadian musician more popularly known as Doctor Music, and who has for a number of years been musical director of the Famous People Players.

A former student at Canada's Royal Conservatory of Music, Riley has made a significant contribution to a wide range of musical genres.

In the folk music genre, **John "Jacko" Reilly**, born in 1926 and who lived for most of his life in Boyle, in Co. Roscommon, was the Irish traditional singer who proved an invaluable source for many of the country's oldest ballads.

Collected and recorded by Tom Munnelly, the songs include *The Raggle Taggle Gypsy* and *The Well Below the Valley*.

Reilly, who died in 1969, learned many of the songs at the feet of his parents, who are thought to have hailed from Carrick-on-Shannon, in Co. Leitrim, but travelled widely throughout the country.

In contemporary times, **Paddy Reilly**, born in Dublin in 1939 is the Irish folk singer and guitarist who is most famously known for his interpretations of the haunting ballads *The Fields of Athenry* and *The Town I Loved So Well*.

A former member of Irish folk band The Dubliners, Reilly is now resident in New York.

Born in Glasgow in 1956, **Maggie Reilly** is the Scottish singer famed for her collaboration in the early 1980s with the composer Mike Oldfield on what have become the classics, *Moonlight Shadow* and *Family Man*.

Despite being interned in Germany for the duration of the Second World War, Canadian-born **Tommy Reilly** went on to become a classical harmonica player and enjoyed a career as a concert soloist and recitalist and a popular performer on British radio and television.

Born in Guelph, Ontario, in 1919, his family moved to London in 1935; on the outbreak of war in 1939 he was a student at the Leipzig Conservatory in Germany, and it was this that led to his internment.

In the world of art, **Frank J. Reilly**, born in 1906 and who died in 1967, was in his lifetime recognised as 'the number one art teacher in America', and is particularly noted by artists for a valuable technique he developed for organising paints on the palette.

A noted contemporary artist is Los Angeles-based **Jack Reilly**, born in 1950, whose uniquely shaped canvas paintings are held in a number of both public and private collections.

An artist of a rather different kind was **Samuel O'Reilly** who, while working as a tattoo artist in New York in 1891, invented and patented the rotary tattoo gun.

Born in Scranton, Pennsylvania, in 1936, **Donald Reilly** was the talented cartoonist whose work appeared in a wide range of magazines that included *The New Yorker*, *Harvard Business Review*, *Playboy*, and *Mad*.

He died in 2006.

Born in Adelaide in 1918, **Pauline Reilly** is a noted Australian ornithologist and author, while **Charles Reilly**, born in London in 1874 was a leading light in British architecture until his death in 1948.

Awarded the Royal Gold Medal for Architecture in 1943, he received a knighthood a year later.

His father, **Charles Reilly**, who was born in 1844 and died in 1928 was also a leading architect and surveyor.

In the world of the popular novel, **Matthew Reilly**, born in Sydney in 1974 is the best-selling Australian writer of action thrillers such as *Ice Station*, *Area T*, and the 2003 *Scarecrow*.

In the highly competitive world of sport, **Bill Riley**, born in Amherst, Nova Scotia, in 1950, is the former Canadian ice hockey player who, at the time of writing, is head coach of the Miramichi Timberwolves of the Maritime Junior A Hockey League.

The third black player in the National Hockey League, Riley played for a number of teams, including the Winnipeg Jets.

On the soccer pitch, **Heather O'Reilly**, born in New Brunswick, New Jersey, in 1985, is the American women's soccer player who helped to take the national team to gold medal victory in the 2004 Olympics in Greece.

On the athletics field, **Ivan Riley**, born in 1900 and who died in 1943, was the American athlete who took the bronze medal for the 400 metre hurdles at the 1924 Olympics in Paris, while **Mike Reilly**, born in Sioux City, Iowa, in 1949, is a celebrated umpire in Major League Baseball.

In the political sphere, **Delbert Riley** is a Canadian First Nations leader; of Chippewa background, he held the position from 1980 to 1982 as chief of the Assembly of First Nations.

The son of Irish immigrants to Canada **James A. Reilly**, born in Naperville, Quebec, in 1835 and who died in 1909, was not only a successful Canadian businessman but also served as Mayor of Alberta on two separate occasions.

Taking to the skies, **James F. Reilly**, born at Mountain Home Air Force base, Idaho, in 1954, is the American astronaut and oil and gas exploration geologist who has flown on two space shuttle missions.

Also on a scientific note, **David Reilly**, born in 1977, is a noted Australian computer scientist and author.

One of the most colourful Reillys was **Lieutenant Sidney George Reilly**, known as the Ace of Spies, who is actually thought to have been born Georgi Rosenblum in about 1874 in Odessa, in the Russian Ukraine.

Thought to have been a model in later years for novelist Ian Fleming's James Bond character, he was a spy extraordinaire and was involved in a number of hair raising escapades on behalf of Britain to overthrow Russia's newly established Bolshevik government.

His dangerous career is thought to have come to a bloody end in November of 1925 when he was executed in a forest near Moscow – but a great deal of speculation and controversy still surround the truth of the matter.

Key dates in Ireland's history from the first settlers to the formation of the Irish Republic:

circa 7000 B.C.	Arrival and settlement of Stone Age people.
circa 3000 B.C.	Arrival of settlers of New Stone Age period.
circa 600 B.C.	First arrival of the Celts.
200 A.D.	Establishment of Hill of Tara, Co. Meath, as seat of the High Kings.
circa 432 A.D.	Christian mission of St. Patrick.
800-920 A.D.	Invasion and subsequent settlement of Vikings.
1002 A.D.	Brian Boru recognised as High King.
1014	Brian Boru killed at battle of Clontarf.
1169-1170	Cambro-Norman invasion of the island.
1171	Henry II claims Ireland for the English Crown.
1366	Statutes of Kilkenny ban marriage between native Irish and English.
1529-1536	England's Henry VIII embarks on religious Reformation.
1536	Earl of Kildare rebels against the Crown.
1541	Henry VIII declared King of Ireland.
1558	Accession to English throne of Elizabeth I.
1565	Battle of Affane.
1569-1573	First Desmond Rebellion.
1579-1583	Second Desmond Rebellion.
1594-1603	Nine Years War.
1606	Plantation' of Scottish and English settlers.

1607	Flight of the Earls.
1632-1636	Annals of the Four Masters compiled.
1641	Rebellion over policy of plantation and other grievances.
1649	Beginning of Cromwellian conquest.
1688	Flight into exile in France of Catholic Stuart monarch James II as Protestant Prince William of Orange invited to take throne of England along with his wife, Mary.
1689	William and Mary enthroned as joint monarchs; siege of Derry.
1690	Jacobite forces of James defeated by William at battle of the Boyne (July) and Dublin taken.
1691	Athlone taken by William; Jacobite defeats follow at Aughrim, Galway, and Limerick; conflict ends with Treaty of Limerick (October) and Irish officers allowed to leave for France.
1695	Penal laws introduced to restrict rights of Catholics; banishment of Catholic clergy.
1704	Laws introduced constricting rights of Catholics in landholding and public office.
1728	Franchise removed from Catholics.
1791	Foundation of United Irishmen republican movement.
1796	French invasion force lands in Bantry Bay.
1798	Defeat of Rising in Wexford and death of United Irishmen leaders Wolfe Tone and Lord Edward Fitzgerald.

1800	Act of Union between England and Ireland.
1803	Dublin Rising under Robert Emmet.
1829	Catholics allowed to sit in Parliament.
1845-1849	The Great Hunger: thousands starve to death as potato crop fails and thousands more emigrate.
1856	Phoenix Society founded.
1858	Irish Republican Brotherhood established.
1873	Foundation of Home Rule League.
1893	Foundation of Gaelic League.
1904	Foundation of Irish Reform Association.
1913	Dublin strikes and lockout.
1916	Easter Rising in Dublin and proclamation of an Irish Republic.
1917	Irish Parliament formed after Sinn Fein election victory.
1919-1921	War between Irish Republican Army and British Army.
1922	Irish Free State founded, while six northern counties remain part of United Kingdom as Northern Ireland, or Ulster; civil war up until 1923 between rival republican groups.
1949	Foundation of Irish Republic after all remaining constitutional links with Britain are severed.